Defending

KU-185-427

Contents

Strong challenge: Tottenham Hotspur defender
Pascal Chimbonda is first to the ball.

INTRODUCTION

Sometimes defenders have to get in where it hurts.

DEFENDERS CAN WIN GAMES, TOO

Winning a game of football is all about goals – scoring more than the opposition. But try looking at it another way … you will win if you concede fewer goals than the opposition.

Study any league table in the world, and you will see that the team with the smallest number in its 'goals against' column will be at the top of the table or close behind. So a successful football team has to have great defenders.

In Italy – a country that has taught the world the value of solid defending – there have been few better central defenders than Fabio Cannavaro or his international teammate Alessandro Nesta. And Paolo Maldini has been an inspiration to a whole generation of Italian youngsters wanting to become full-backs.

Spanish kids have looked up to Fernando Hierro, the French to Lillian Thuram and Marcel Desailly. In the English Premiership, the likes of Rio Ferdinand and John Terry are idols.

But even forwards need to have the basic skills of defending. All good teams 'defend from the front'.

This means that, when they lose the ball, teams must get players between their own goal and the ball. So, your team's attackers are also your first line of defence.

It doesn't matter where you play on the pitch, you have to be a good defender, with a grasp of the necessary skills – tackling, marking and passing.

We all marvel at the attacking flair of players like Welsh wing-wizard Ryan Giggs, Italy's Francesco Totti and Frenchman Thierry Henry. We admire the all-round talents of Steven Gerrard and the agility of a host of goalkeepers.

But defenders can be just as skilled – and just as important to the end result. The following chapters will show you how.

It's mine! Eyes on the ball, good balance and determination are needed to win the tackle.

3

Defenders come in all shapes and sizes. They are not all giants with thighs like tree-trunks and the flattest of foreheads. Height and bulk helps if you are playing in central defence – and having to mark a bull of a centre-forward like Brazilian superstar Ronaldo or Christian Vieri, of Italy.

Some central strikers are fast. France's Thierry Henry and England's Michael Owen have pace to spare when it comes to taking on defenders. So speed on the turn, speed of thought (anticipation) and positioning, are just as important.

Full-backs must be able to head the ball against taller opponents. And they can win it, if their technique and timing is right.

Defenders need a whole range of qualities. The box below gives a list. Some are fairly obvious, and many apply if you are to be successful in any position on the pitch.

But there are specialist areas, like heading the ball for distance to clear your lines, and tackling without the ball falling free to another attacker.

Keep calm: Good control and vision are key assets.

WHAT MAKES A GOOD DEFENDER?

- Calm under pressure
- Confidence
- Courage
- Quick reactions
- Being decisive
- Ability to 'read' the game

Getting shirty: Brazil's Roberto Carlos, right, tackles a German forward.

We will look at these areas in greater detail in the following chapters. You will also improve if you watch and learn from better players. Look how much time good players seem to have on the ball – that is no accident. They do it by making sure they are always in the right position, and watching for dangers before they happen.

Defending is sometimes uncomfortable – attackers will be forceful in trying to get to the ball ahead of you.

Courage and strength are key. Defenders don't always get the credit they deserve – just the complaints when the ball ends up in your net!

TACKLING

To win games, a team needs to score goals. But, in order to score a goal, you have to have the ball. You can't score while the other side has it.

The more possession you have, the better your chances of scoring. You can win the ball from the opposition by picking up a pass that goes astray, or being first to a loose clearance, or you can tackle the player with the ball.

Tackling is an explosive action. But a smart defender will be patient and not dive in. There is nothing more embarrassing than being left on the floor, looking back as an attacker runs on to score!

You need to choose your moment – often when the attacker has knocked the ball a little too far to be in control of it. You will also need to keep him guessing about when you will challenge.

Here are some drills that will set you on the way to becoming a good tackling defender.

PRACTICE NO.1

This is what I call the rope trick. You need two players and a metre-long piece of rope, or string. Even a training top will do.

- The attacker holds the rope facing the defender, and allows the end of the rope to touch the floor, just in front of the defender.

- The defender pounces forward to try to stamp on, or touch, the rope before the attacker can drag it away. This will test your reflexes!

- Allow the defender to have five attempts, then swap positions.

GO FOR IT!

Any movement of any part of the defender's body will alert the attacker to whip the rope away.

Rope trick: Whip the top or piece of string away while your pal tries to step on it.

BE THE BEST

The best posture for a defender is to stand with legs slightly bent at the knees, feet shoulder-width apart. The body should be leaning forward slightly. You should feel balanced and ready to move in any direction.

PRACTICE NO. 2

Let's make things more realistic. Mark out a pitch as shown in the diagram. Make each goal three paces wide. Use cones if you have them, though jumpers will do. Two of you are needed for this drill.

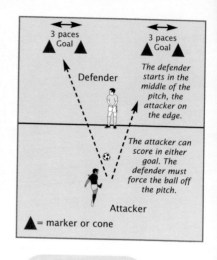

3 paces
Goal

3 paces
Goal

Defender

The defender starts in the middle of the pitch, the attacker on the edge.

The attacker can score in either goal. The defender must force the ball off the pitch.

Attacker

▲ = marker or cone

- An attacker starts with a ball on the edge of the pitch. The defender starts in the middle of the pitch. The attacker has five attempts to score in either goal.

- The defender must attempt to win the ball and force it off the pitch.

- After five attempts, change over.

- Keep your scores. Play three rounds in total to see who is the winner.

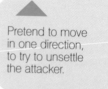

Pretend to move in one direction, to try to unsettle the attacker.

BE THE BEST

The defender should be patient – don't dive in! Stay on your feet and see if you can work out which way the attacker is going to move. The best time to challenge is when he does not have the ball fully under control.

HEADING FOR **DEFENDERS**

Generally, when you are in the penalty area and need to clear the ball with your head, you need to get as much distance on the header as you can. All too often weak clearances are picked up around the penalty area and smashed into the back of the net by hungry forwards!

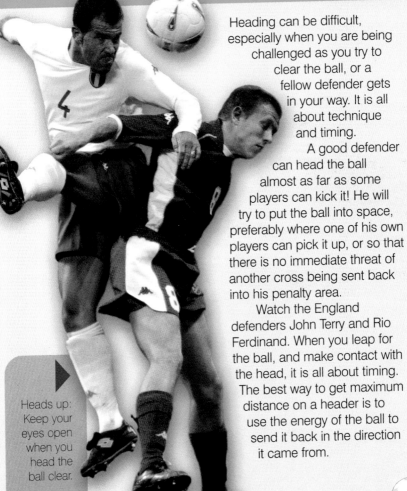

Heading can be difficult, especially when you are being challenged as you try to clear the ball, or a fellow defender gets in your way. It is all about technique and timing.

A good defender can head the ball almost as far as some players can kick it! He will try to put the ball into space, preferably where one of his own players can pick it up, or so that there is no immediate threat of another cross being sent back into his penalty area.

Watch the England defenders John Terry and Rio Ferdinand. When you leap for the ball, and make contact with the head, it is all about timing. The best way to get maximum distance on a header is to use the energy of the ball to send it back in the direction it came from.

Heads up: Keep your eyes open when you head the ball clear.

PRACTICE NO. 1

For this drill, you will need two players and one ball. Mark out a small pitch, five paces long, with a goal three paces wide.

- An attacker stands with a ball in the middle of the pitch. He 'serves' the ball with his hands – just toss it up – so the defender can head it back over the attacker's head.

- The defender should try to score in the goal (this is a special goal – the cross bar is as high as the moon!) Height and distance are the aims of this exercise.

- If the defender scores without the ball bouncing, he receives a bonus point.

- The attacker can try to prevent the goal by using his hands, like a goalkeeper.

- Have five goes each, then swap positions, but don't accept a poor serve that you can't head decently.

BE THE BEST

- **Head through the bottom half of the ball. This will send it high.**
- **Attack the ball – be aggressive. This will give the ball distance.**

Tip: Keep your mouth closed to avoid biting your tongue.

Practice: Head it back at the server.

FURTHER PRACTICE

Make a pitch 12 paces long.

- The defender can run from outside the area to head the ball.

- The same rules apply as before.

GO FOR IT!

Try leaping from just one foot. Arch your back and neck, and attack the ball.

BE THE BEST

- Swing your arms in an upward motion to help you gain height. Be careful not to handle the ball.

- As you are in the air, bend your knees and lift your ankles up towards your behind.

Now extend the pitch to 15 paces.

- The attacker serves the ball, either with a drop-kick from his hands (volley), or from the ground.

- The attacker serves from the goal. Remember, this goal has no crossbar, so you can head it as high as you like.

- Have five goes each and keep score.

11

CONTROLLING THE **BALL**

A defender often has to clear the ball first time in desperate situations. But there are occasions when he or she becomes the first point of attack.

It is then that the defender must be able to bring the ball under control before delivering a precise pass. The best defenders have excellent ball control. No matter what height the ball comes to them, they can master it in a moment. Here is a mental image which will help you to understand more clearly: if you put a blanket over a washing line and then kicked the ball at the blanket, what would happen?

- The ball would hit the blanket and drop motionless to the ground.

- Why? Because the blanket absorbs all the energy of the ball by 'cushioning' it, caving in at the moment of impact and absorbing that impact.

If you want to 'kill' the ball then the part of the body that meets it must behave like the blanket and absorb all the energy of the ball, no matter what height.

GO FOR IT!

**Remember!
Cushion the ball like
a blanket.**

Chest-trap: Don't push your chest at the ball. Pull it away at impact so that the ball drops at your feet.

PRACTICE NO. 1

Set up a narrow pitch with goals three paces wide. You need two players and one ball. Both of you stand in a goal.

- Using an underarm throw, try to score in the other goal. The ball cannot go above head height.

- Each player gains a point by preventing the goal, and controlling the ball before it moves one pace away. You cannot use your arms or hands!

- Have ten throws each.

- The winner is the player who secures the ball the most number of times.

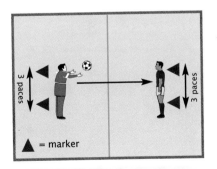

3 paces

3 paces

▲ = marker

Practice No. 1.

PASSING THE **BALL**

If you thought passing was a skill best left to the creative geniuses, think again. It is a skill defenders need, too. You have already found out that the defender can be the first line of attack as he brings the ball out of defence, or if he wins a tackle and finds the ball at his feet.

Pass it right: Use the instep to send an accurate long pass, though you can also use the outside of your foot to apply 'bend' or spin.

A good, accurate pass is essential if the attack is not to break down straight away. Also, a poor pass, straight to an opposing attacker, can leave your own defence wide open.

Passing is about keeping possession, and it is very much linked to the subject of the last chapter – control. Once you have comfortably secured the ball, you must then deliver an accurate pass to one of your team.

Defenders should generally pass to their teammates' feet, rather than into space ahead of them. Defenders have the advantage of being able to look ahead to see play develop in front of them, while attackers often receive the ball with their backs to goal.

However, the most important point to stress is that losing possession close to your own goal is a recipe for disaster. That is why the defender must concentrate fully, in order to be accurate with his pass.

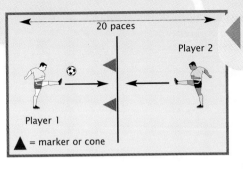

20 paces

Player 2

Player 1

▲ = marker or cone

Take turns to pass through markers just one pace apart.

PRACTICE NO. 1

Set up a pitch as shown. You will need two players and one ball for this exercise.

- Each player stands 10 paces from a goal just one pace wide in the middle of the pitch.

- Each player has 10 attempts to score by passing the ball through the tiny goal.

- Try five passes with the left foot, five with the right foot.

- The goal will be disallowed unless the ball goes through the goal and reaches the other player.

- Have ten goes each. Keep your score: the winner is the player with most goals.

BE THE BEST

When you strike the ball, try to follow through with your foot in the direction of the goal.

Brazilian defender Roberto Carlos shows that good passing is a skill defenders also have to master.

Try using your left foot and your right foot in turns to pass the ball. It will help make you a better player.

PRACTICE NO. 2

Three attackers take on one defender.

- Only one attacker can be on the pitch, along with the lone defender. The other attackers can move along the sidelines, and call for a pass, but they cannot go on to the pitch.

- The attacker on the pitch must score a goal after passing to one of the other attackers and collecting the return pass.

- A goal is wiped out each time the defender intercepts the ball. When he does so, he should give the ball back and play restarts. Each game lasts for two minutes. Then change positions.

- The attackers must all work hard to collect a pass. The attacker on the pitch can run in any direction to fool the defender.

GO FOR IT!

Try passing the ball into one of the tiny goals with your first touch.

Practice No. 2.

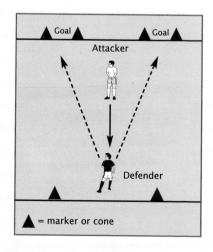

PRESSING THE **BALL**

When an opponent has the ball, your role as a defender means you must try to prevent him:

- passing the ball forward to a fellow team player
- having a shot at goal
- moving forward with the ball.

The key in each case is to get close to the attacker as quickly as possible, and then assess the situation again. You must not give the attacker room to move, or time to think about his options. We call this 'closing down the space', or pressing.

The best defenders, like Spain's Fernando Hierro and England full-back Ashley Cole, who is especially quick, close down the space in an instant. Poor defenders complain to their teammates, while an attacker nips between them and the ball rests in the back of their net!

Quick step: Get to the player with the ball as quickly as you can, to stop him making the most of the space and time he has to create danger for your team.

GO FOR IT!

Sprint quickly once you have passed the ball. When you get close to the attacker, slow right down.

Try to prevent as many goals as possible.

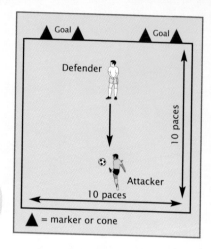

Goal

Goal

Defender

10 paces

Attacker

10 paces

▲ = marker or cone

PRACTICE NO. 1

This drill will get you into the habit of 'closing the space down' quickly. Set up a pitch 10 paces square. Add a couple of goals, as shown in the diagram.

- The defender starts on the line with the ball and passes it firmly to the attacker.

- The attacker must have a minimum of two touches, and a maximum of three, to score in either of the two small goals.

- The defender should sprint forward to prevent the goal attempt.

- Have five attempts each, then try another five. Keep your score. The winner is the defender who prevents most goals.

PRACTICE NO. 2

Use a pitch 10 paces square with a goal at one end, four paces wide.

- The defender makes a firm pass to the attacker, and must then close the space down quickly.

- This time, make your run slightly curved. The attacker will probably move away from you instead of towards you – a natural response!

- You have started to dictate the attacker's moves and take control. Now try to guide him in one direction.

- Have five goes each, then another set of five. The winner is the one who prevents most goals.

When you get to the attacker, don't dive in to tackle. Let him make a mistake and lose full control of the ball, then make the tackle.

COVERING YOUR **MATES**

Football is a team game – but you don't just do things as one 11-player unit. There are at least three mini-teams working together in different areas of the pitch to make the whole team successful.

Outnumbered: As soon as the striker gets the ball, he's faced by a defender and one of his teammates.

The backline will work together, talking to, and covering for, each other. So will the midfield and the forwards. If all the mini-teams are working well, then the team as a whole will do well.

There are situations on the pitch when you need to 'back-up' your teammate, who might be struggling to cope with a tough opponent, or he may be outnumbered. That is when it is your duty to give him a hand. Assess the situation quickly to see where you need to be in order to help your teammate out best.

If England's Wayne Rooney is about to take on a defender, you can bet that the defender's nearest teammates will be there to offer their support.

DID YOU KNOW?

Former Arsenal defender Tony Adams made his England debut against Spain in 1987, alongside Glenn Hoddle. He later captained the England side managed by Hoddle.

PRACTICE NO. 1

Mark a pitch 10 paces wide by 20 paces long, with goals four paces wide at either end. Two defenders take on one attacker.

- The defenders line up on the goal-line and one of them kicks the ball firmly to the attacker to start play.
- The attacker should attempt to dribble the ball through the defenders' goal.
- The defenders try to win the ball and dribble it through the attacker's goal.
- Have five goes, then each player changes position. The defenders who score most goals are the winners.

BE THE BEST

One defender should make a fast, curved approach to the ball. Get sideways on to the attacker, 'inviting' him to move towards his 'trap'. The second defender should cover his teammate. It means the first defender can afford to make a tackle, with his teammate ready to steal the ball if it runs loose.

GO FOR IT!

Defenders should be on the 'balls of their feet'. A quick attacker can race past a defender who is back on his heels.

Waiting game: Don't dive in to challenge. Wait for the attacker to lose control of the ball.

Solid tackle: As soon as the attacker looks to have lost control, get in a strong challenge to win the ball.

PRACTICE NO. 2

This drill pits two attackers against two defenders on a pitch about 30 paces long.

- The defenders start together at one end, and the attackers start together at the other.

- The game starts when the first defender passes the ball to either of the attackers.

- The game is over when the attackers have dribbled the ball over the goal-line, or have lost possession.

- Have five starts, then change roles.

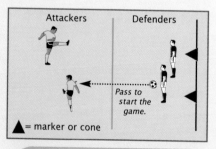

Attackers   Defenders

Pass to start the game.

▲ = marker or cone

The defenders must cover each other in this practice.

BE THE BEST

Be patient. If you miss a tackle, make a quick recovery behind your teammate, who is covering you!

STOP AN OPPONENT **TURNING**

When a forward receives the ball with his back to goal, it is important that he is not allowed to turn and attack. As a defender, you have a big advantage. You are already standing between the attacker and your goal, and he is facing the wrong way. But it can all change in a moment. You have to be on your guard.

If players like Didier Drogba or Wayne Rooney are allowed to turn with the ball, they can cause chaos for the opposing team.

It is vital that defenders concentrate at all times, and are ready to close down an attacker to stop him from turning.

DID YOU KNOW?

Fernando Hierro became Spain's all-time top goalscorer, despite being a defender. He played in four World Cups and was an expert at long-range free-kicks. Hierro won European Cup glory with Real Madrid.

Make it tough: Don't give the forward (the player in blue) room to turn.

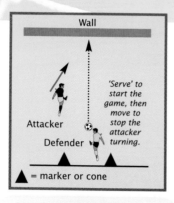

Wall

'Serve' to start the game, then move to stop the attacker turning.

Attacker

Defender

 = marker or cone

Move to collect the ball when it comes off the wall, then turn to attack the goal.

BE THE BEST

- Make up the ground quickly, but stop about one pace from the attacker.
- Stoop down low so that you can see the ball from behind the attacker.
- Keep alert and on your toes, and make it difficult for the attacker to turn.

PRACTICE NO. 1

For this practice you will need two players. You can use a wall – or another friend – to be the server.

- The attacker stands 10 paces from the wall. The defender starts with the ball 15 paces from the wall.

- The defender serves the ball by passing it firmly against the wall so that it rebounds to the attacker. The moment the ball hits the wall, both players are 'live'.

- The attacker has 10 seconds to try to dribble or pass the ball between the two markers.

- Have five goes each, and then repeat twice more. The winner is the defender who prevents most goals.

GO FOR IT!

Don't get too close to the attacker, or he could roll his body against yours and turn.

Be alert: The defender (shown in red) is watching the ball, being ready to tackle or prevent the attacker from passing.

Lean round the attacker to make sure you get a clear sight of the ball.

PRACTICE NO. 2

Set up a pitch 20 paces long, with a goal at each end six paces wide. This is a two-a-side game. Each team has a defender and an attacker. You will need to mark a half-way line.

- Attackers play in their opponents' half, defenders in their own half. No player may cross the halfway line (see diagram below).

- A defender must remain between the opposing attacker and the goal, unless his own attacker has the ball.

- When his attacker has possession, he can 'support' him by getting ahead of the attacker he is marking to receive a pass, but he must stay in his own half.

- As soon as his attacker loses possession, he must ignore the ball and go back to his position behind the opposing attacker.

- The game is over when either team scores, or the ball leaves the pitch.

- Each team has five starts, then change roles with your teammate, and start again.

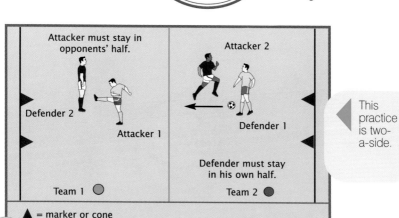

Attacker must stay in opponents' half.

Attacker 2

Defender 2

Attacker 1

Defender 1

Defender must stay in his own half.

Team 1 ○   Team 2 ●

This practice is two-a-side.

▲ = marker or cone

26

CLEARANCES AND **VOLLEYS**

Playing football is about making decisions. Making the wrong decision on the pitch can have disastrous results! If a defender makes the wrong decision, it can often result in a goal against his team.

Plenty of goals come from defensive errors. Watch a game in your local park or on TV. Think about how a goal was scored. It isn't always down to the individual brilliance of an attacker…

When a defender is under pressure from an attacker he has to clear the ball. Often a defender will try to pass his way out of trouble when a good booted clearance upfield would be a better bet. The best defenders do not take chances!

There is an old saying in football: 'When in doubt – out!' In other words, if you are unsure what to do, always go for the safest option – the big, booted clearance. In this section, there are two drills designed to give you the feel and confidence of striking the ball.

Good volley:
Perfect balance,
eye on the ball.

PRACTICE NO. 1

You need a big area for this practice – well away from buildings with windows!

- Stand no more than one pace from the goal-line of a goal with a net, or one pace from a washing line with a heavy blanket firmly secured to it.

- Hold the ball in your hands, let it drop to the ground, and strike the ball forward. Have ten goes.

BE THE BEST

- Strike the ball with the laced part of your boot.

- Strike through the bottom half of the ball, not right underneath it.

Power play: volley the ball as hard as you can.

GO FOR IT!

Keep your eyes on the ball as you make contact.

Portsmouth's Matthew Taylor concentrates as he volleys the ball.

PRACTICE NO. 2

Stand one pace away from a goal or blanket, and turn sideways.

- A partner, no more than three paces away, serves you a ball from their hands. The serve should not be above knee-height.

- Volley the ball into the goal or blanket using your right foot. Have five goes.

GO FOR IT!

Your shoulders should be falling backwards slightly as you strike the ball.

- Your partner then serves from the other side, so that you can practise with your left foot.

COUNTERATTACKING

We have looked at clearing the ball while under pressure from an opponent. But if a defender is not under pressure he can bring the ball under control and start a counterattack.

A defender can also use the counterattack if he breaks up an attack with an interception or tackle. Rio Ferdinand of England and Sami Hyypia, Liverpool's Finnish defender, are very good at setting up counterattacks. Watch games to see how confidently such players bring the ball out of defence. They don't look down at the ball – they look ahead for teammates. Quite often, the other team will back off, giving the defender more time and space than they would give to an opposing forward.

A counterattack should be swift and direct, leaving the opposition players stranded!

PRACTICE NO. 1

Two defenders v two attackers. They line up in each half of a small pitch (see diagram on page 31). The defenders must stay in their half.

• The attackers try to run the ball across the defenders' goal line – they can't just kick it over, but they can pass to each other.

• The defenders try to win the ball. If they do, they should attack quickly, trying to run the ball into the other goal (don't just boot it).

• If the attackers lose the ball, they must run back to defend their goal.

• When a goal is scored, or the ball goes off the pitch, the attackers start again with the ball.

• One game lasts three minutes. Then change teams.

BE THE BEST

• The defenders should try hard to anticipate the attackers' passes.
• A defender's pass to his teammate should be quick and accurate.

Defenders

Attackers

*Attack one end first,
then the other.*

▲ = marker or cone

Win the ball,
then bring it out
of defence and
pass it to the
the attacker.

Perfect poise:
Look ahead at
how the game is
opening up – not
down at the ball
– when you start
a counterattack.

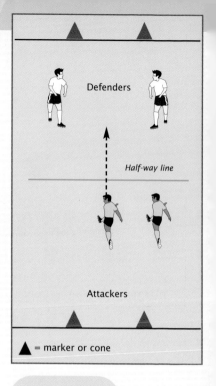

= marker or cone

 Practice No. 2.

GO FOR IT!

It is unsafe to counterattack, then 'clear your lines' – get the ball off the pitch!

PRACTICE NO. 2

This practice is an extension of the last one. Two attackers against two defenders.

- To score, the attackers must dribble the ball across the goal-line – not shoot at the goal.

- If the defenders win the ball, they should try to score in the opposite goal by dribbling the ball across the line as before. But only one defender may cross the half-way line with the ball at any time.

- One defender should make a fast break into the other half, while the one with the ball looks to pass it to him.

- The game lasts for three minutes, then reverse roles.

- Keep score – the team with the best goal-difference will be the winner.

BE THE BEST

- When the defenders win the ball, they should react quickly.

- The defenders should talk to each other at all times. Let your teammate know where you are.

No way past: Jonathan Woodgate of Middlesborough stands firm against Ryan Giggs.